AF595796

For Lucie
May you always gaze in wonder
at all the critters above and under

—Amandine Thomas

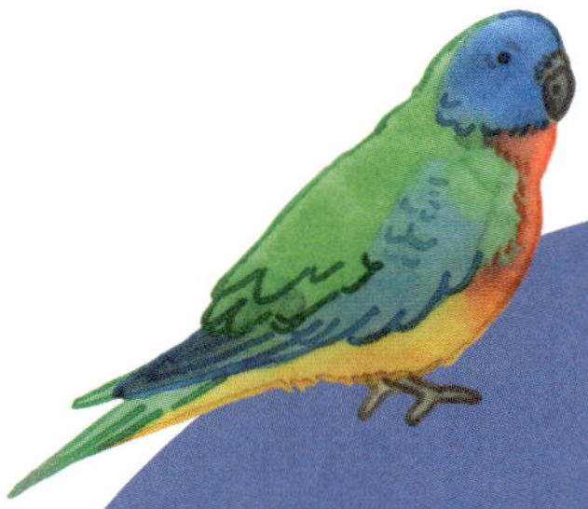

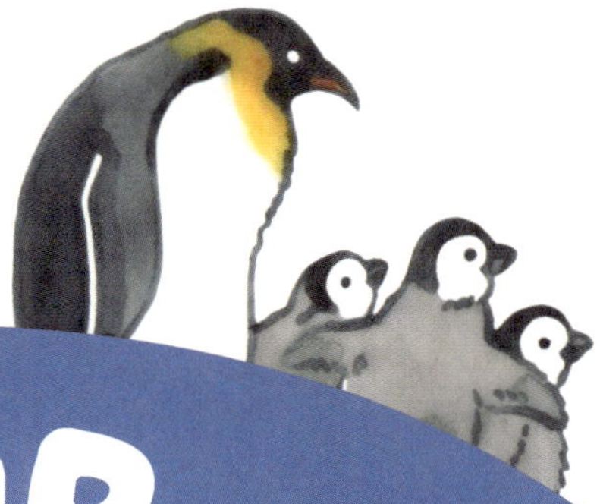

OUR WONDROUS PLANET

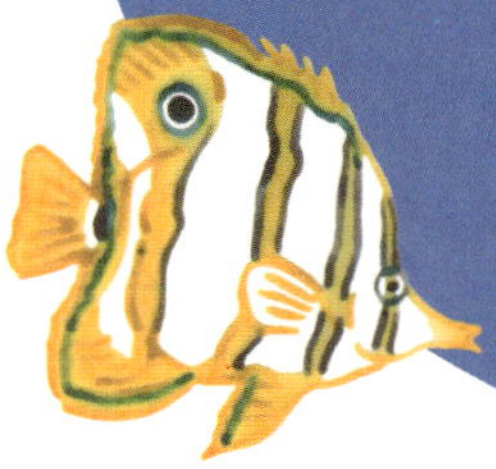

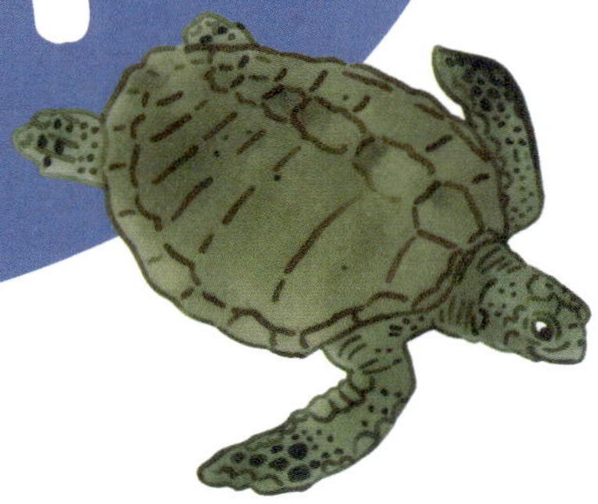

A SEARCH-AND-FIND ADVENTURE

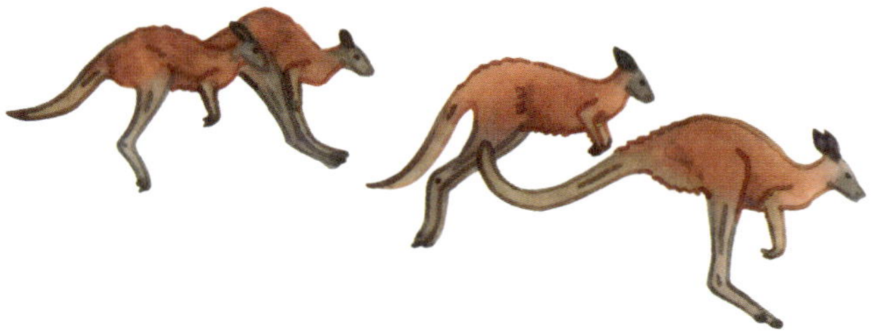

Illustrated by
Amandine Thomas

EXPLORING OUR WONDROUS PLANET

Earth is the only planet we know with life. This makes it very special.

Living things can be found everywhere—from the tops of mountains to the deepest parts of the ocean, from harsh deserts to lush rainforests. Animals, plants, fungi and tiny microbes have special features that help them survive in these very different places.

If we look around the Earth, we can see that some places have the same kind of climate. Because of this, they also have similar environments where certain types of plants and animals thrive. These areas, where particular climates support particular living things, are called **biomes.**

There are five major types of biomes across the world: **AQUATIC, GRASSLAND, FOREST, DESERT** and **TUNDRA.**

Within each of these five major biome types there are all kinds of subcategories. For example, Victorian bushland is very different to Queensland's tropical rainforests, but both of these habitats are a type of forest.

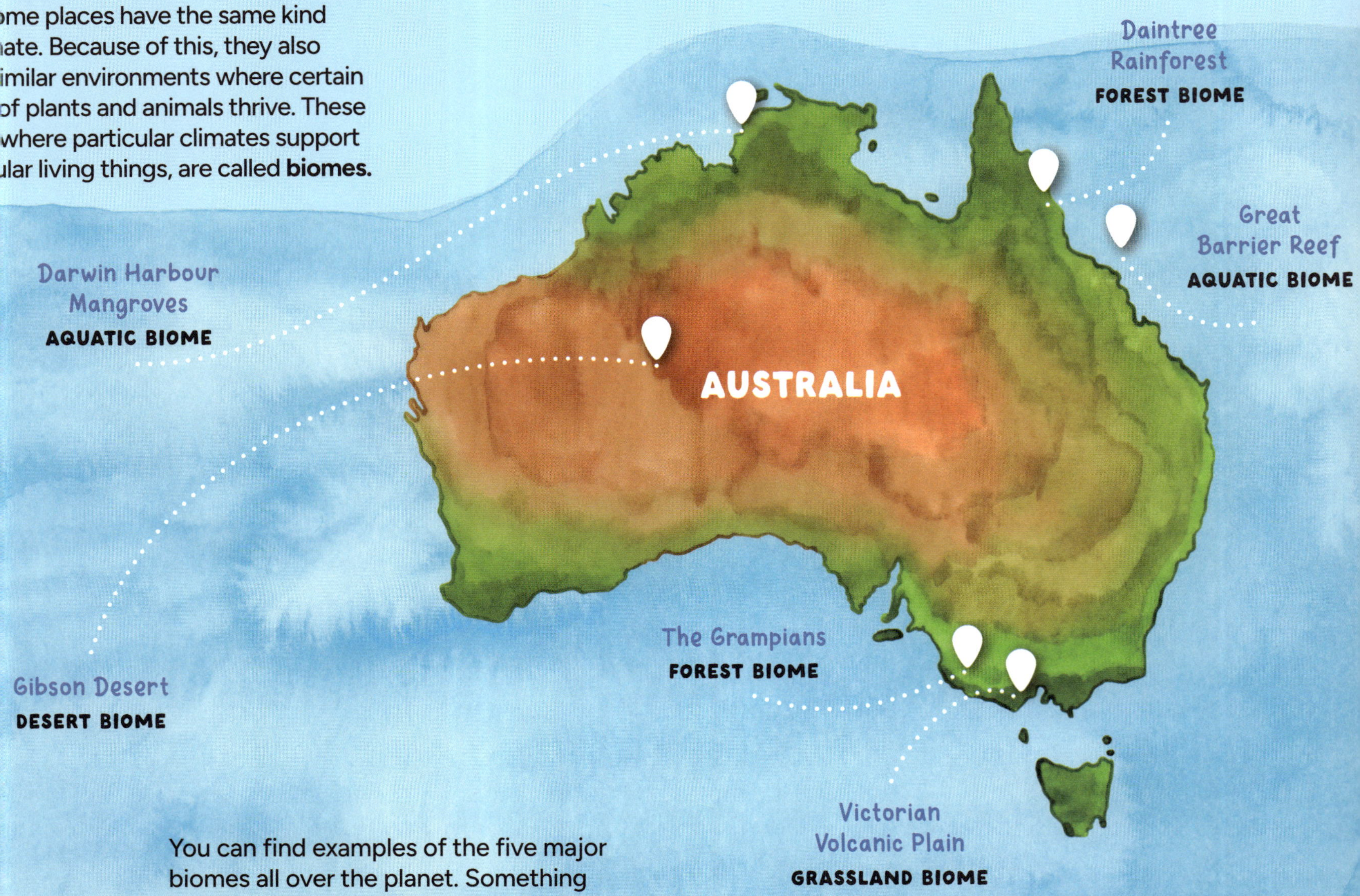

Daintree Rainforest
FOREST BIOME

Great Barrier Reef
AQUATIC BIOME

Darwin Harbour Mangroves
AQUATIC BIOME

AUSTRALIA

The Grampians
FOREST BIOME

Gibson Desert
DESERT BIOME

Victorian Volcanic Plain
GRASSLAND BIOME

You can find examples of the five major biomes all over the planet. Something special about Australia is that it contains almost all of the key biomes! The one exception is the icy tundra, which is found to the south of Australia on the Antarctic Peninsula.

ANTARCTICA
TUNDRA BIOME

In this book, you'll go on an adventure through eight amazing environments to find animals big and small. Keep an eye out for creatures hidden in the **Daintree Rainforest**, the **Great Barrier Reef**, the **Gibson Desert**, the **Victorian Volcanic Plain**, **Antarctica**, the **Darwin Harbour mangroves**, the Australian **soil** and the **Grampians**.

Can you find all the hidden animals? You might spot some quickly, but for others you'll need to use your powers of observation! Keep looking—you never know what unexpected details you'll uncover.

DAINTREE RAINFOREST

In the Daintree Rainforest, steady rain and humidity fuel an explosion of life and colour that stretches from the tops of the trees down to their sturdy buttress roots.

Millions of animals and plants coexist in this richly layered habitat, from the majestic Hercules Moth to the elusive Cassowary. The forest is humming with life!

Northern Long-nosed Bandicoot

Prickly Katydid

Lesser Sooty Owl

Green Ringtail Possum

Black-eared Catbird

Eastern Tube-nosed Bat

Spotted Tree Monitor

Northern Barred Frog

Peppermint Stick Insect

Green Python

GREAT BARRIER REEF

In the tropical waters of the Great Barrier Reef, coral forms a colourful living home for an astounding diversity of life. Coral reefs are home to a quarter of all marine life on Earth. From the littlest Sea Cucumber to the large, gentle Whale Shark, everyone plays a role in life on the reef.

Ridged Swimmer Crab
Greater Blue-ringed Octopus
Bullock's Hypselodoris
Green Sea Turtle
Yellow Coralgoby
Banded Wobbegong
Eastern Clown Anemonefish

GIBSON DESERT

In the Gibson Desert, plants and animals have had to adapt to extreme temperatures and low rainfall in order to thrive.

Amongst the gravel, red sand and hardy vegetation, a surprising array of animals make their homes above and below ground.

Lesser Hairy-footed Dunnart

Night Parrot

Great Desert Skink

Western Bearded Dragon

Perentie

Woma

Spotted Nightjar

VICTORIAN VOLCANIC PLAIN

The grasslands, wetlands and rocky rises of the Victorian Volcanic Plain are home to a range of incredible—and rare—plants and animals.

Ancient volcanic activity helped make this the perfect environment for many unique animals, who make their homes amongst the native grasses and flowers.

Spotted Marsh Frog
Short-beaked Echidna
Plains-wanderer
Tawny Frogmouth
Eastern Yellow Robin
Victorian Grassland Earless Dragon
Little Whip Snake

DARWIN HARBOUR MANGROVES

Mangrove communities, like the ones in Darwin Harbour, are an important ecosystem teeming with rich biodiversity. Growing along the coastline where the salty seawater meets land, mangroves have evolved to become a unique home for wildlife. They are feeding and nesting sites for migratory birds, and nurseries for fish.

Little Red Flying-fox
Thin Periwinkle
Mangrove Monitor
Giant Mud Crab
Hooded Katydid
Darwin's Mudskipper
Black-ringed Mangrove Sea Snake

ANTARCTICA

In the freezing waters to the south of Australia, there is abundant life on the world's driest continent—the icy landscape of Antarctica.

Many kinds of animals—from birds to mammals to fish—have adapted to survive on harsh rocky outcrops, vast ice sheets and icy deserts, and in the freezing ocean.

Unicorn Icefish

Antarctic Tern

Macaroni Penguin

Crabeater Seal

Snowy Sheathbill

Leopard Seal
Imperial Cormorant

SOIL

A dynamic underground life support system thrives beneath our feet. Sharing is everything in this underground community we call soil.

Plants, fungi and microbes combine their talents in sprawling networks pulsing with nutrients to keep the most species-rich habitat on Earth alive. There's a whole world down below your feet!

Sugar Ant

Red Velvet Mite

Black Portuguese Millipede

Pobblebonk

Striped Legless Lizard

Greengrocer Cicada

Common Slater

THE GRAMPIANS

The temperate forest of the Grampians (Gariwerd) National Park is resplendent with flowers and plants that are unique to this place and thrive in its dry soil.

Against the backdrop of sweeping slopes, rocky outcrops, flowing water and plentiful plants, an abundant array of wildlife can be found.

Spotted Pardalote

Lace Monitor

Wedge-tailed Eagle

Eastern Pygmy Possum

Smoky Mouse

Rainbow Lorikeet

Common Brush-tailed Possum

Eastern Bearded Dragon

Tiger Snake

White-striped Free-tailed Bat

DAINTREE RAINFOREST

1. **Spotted Tree Monitor *(Varanus scalaris)***
2. Rainbow Bee-eater *(Merops ornatus)*
3. Spectacled Flying-fox *(Pteropus conspicillatus)*
4. Bennett's Tree Kangaroo *(Dendrolagus bennettianus)*
5. Double-eyed Fig-parrot *(Cyclopsitta diophthalma)*
6. **Eastern Tube-nosed Bat *(Nyctimene robinsoni)***
7. Superb Fruit-dove *(Ptilinopus superbus)*
8. Boyd's Forest Dragon *(Lophosaurus boydii)*
9. **Green Ringtail Possum *(Pseudochirops archeri)***
10. Palm Cockatoo *(Probosciger aterrimus)*
11. **Green Python *(Morelia viridis)***
12. Ulysses Butterfly *(Papilio ulysses)*
13. Buff-breasted Paradise Kingfisher *(Tanysiptera sylvia)*
14. **Lesser Sooty Owl *(Tyto tenebricosa)***
15. Southern Cassowary *(Casuarius casuarius)*
16. Hercules Moth *(Coscinocera hercules)*
17. **Black-eared Catbird *(Ailuroedus melanotis)***
18. Common Striped Possum *(Dactylopsila trivirgata)*
19. Spotted-tailed Quoll *(Dasyurus maculatus)*
20. **Northern Long-nosed Bandicoot *(Perameles pallescens)***
21. White-lipped Tree Frog *(Litoria infrafrenata)*
22. Graceful Honeyeater *(Meliphaga gracilis)*
23. Victoria's Riflebird *(Ptiloris victoriae)*
24. **Peppermint Stick Insect *(Megacrania batesii)***
25. Musky Rat-kangaroo *(Hypsiprymnodon moschatus)*
26. Cairns Birdwing Butterfly *(Ornithoptera euphorion)*
27. **Northern Barred Frog *(Mixophyes schevilli)***
28. Fire-tailed Skink *(Morethia taeniopleura)*
29. Green Tree Ant *(Oecophylla smaragdina)*
30. Australian Rhinoceros Beetle *(Xylotrupes australicus)*
31. Four O'clock Moth *(Dysphania numana)*
32. **Prickly Katydid *(Phricta spinosa)***

GREAT BARRIER REEF

1. Tiger Shark *(Galeocerdo cuvier)*
2. **Eastern Clown Anemonefish *(Amphiprion percula)***
3. Potato Rockcod *(Epinephelus tukula)*
4. Whale Shark *(Rhincodon typus)*
5. Golden Trevally *(Gnathanodon speciosus)* – juvenile
6. Persian Carpet Flatworm *(Pseudobiceros bedfordi)*
7. Trumpet Triton *(Charonia tritonis)*
8. Hawksbill Sea Turtle *(Eretmochelys imbricata)*
9. Dugong *(Dugong dugon)*
10. Manta Ray *(Mobula alfredi)*
11. **Green Sea Turtle *(Chelonia mydas)***
12. Feather Star *(Tropiometra afra)*
13. Australian Snubfin Dolphin *(Orcaella heinsohni)*
14. Humphead Maori Wrasse *(Cheilinus undulatus)*
15. Yellowback Fusilier *(Caesio xanthonotus)*
16. Emperor Angelfish *(Pomacanthus imperator)*
17. Helfrichi Dartfish *(Nemateleotris helfrichi)*
18. **Long Leg Rock Lobster *(Panulirus longipes)***
19. Beaked Coralfish *(Chelmon rostratus)*
20. Violetline Parrotfish *(Scarus globiceps)*
21. **Day Octopus *(Octopus cyanea)***
22. **Boring Clam *(Tridacna crocea)***
23. **Bullock's Hypselodoris *(Hypselodoris bullockii)***
24. **Ridged Swimmer Crab *(Charybdis natator)***
25. White-patch Nautilus *(Nautilus stenomphalus)*
26. **Greater Blue-ringed Octopus *(Hapalochlaena lunulata)***
27. **Banded Wobbegong *(Orectolobus ornatus)***
28. Leopard Sea Cucumber *(Bohadschia argus)*
29. Peacock Mantis Shrimp *(Odontodactylus scyllarus)*
30. **Yellow Coralgoby *(Gobiodon okinawae)***

GIBSON DESERT

1. Pink Cockatoo (*Cacatua leadbeateri*)
2. Emu (*Dromaius novaehollandiae*)
3. Red Kangaroo (*Osphranter rufus*)
4. Sand Goanna (*Varanus gouldii*)
5. Striated Pardalote (*Pardalotus striatus*)
6. Black-flanked Rock Wallaby (*Petrogale lateralis*)
7. **Perentie (*Varanus giganteus*)**
8. Dingo (*Canis familiaris*)
9. Malleefowl (*Leipoa ocellata*)
10. Princess Parrot (*Polytelis alexandrae*)
11. Scarlet-chested Parrot (*Neophema splendida*)
12. **Woma (*Aspidites ramsayi*)**
13. Greater Bilby (*Macrotis lagotis*)
14. Centralian Bluetongue (*Tiliqua multifasciata*)
15. Brush-tailed Bettong (*Bettongia penicillata*)
16. Southern Marsupial Mole (*Notoryctes typhlops*)
17. **Lesser Hairy-footed Dunnart (*Sminthopsis youngsoni*)**
18. **Spotted Nightjar (*Eurostopodus argus*)**
19. Brush-tailed Mulgara (*Dasycercus blythi*)
20. **Western Bearded Dragon (*Pogona minor*)**
21. **Night Parrot (*Pezoporus occidentalis*)**
22. **Great Desert Skink (*Liopholis kintorei*)**
23. **Southern Sandslider (*Lerista labialis*)**
24. Pale Knob-tailed Gecko (*Nephrurus laevissimus*)
25. Bynoe's Gecko (*Heteronotia binoei*)
26. Burton's Legless Lizard (*Lialis burtonis*)
27. Central Deserts Robust Slider (*Lerista desertorum*)
28. **Spinifex Hopping Mouse (*Notomys alexis*)**
29. Thorny Devil (*Moloch horridus*)
30. **Long-tailed Dunnart (*Antechinomys longicaudatus*)**

VICTORIAN VOLCANIC PLAIN

1. Black-shouldered Kite (*Elanus axillaris*)
2. Galah (*Eolophus roseicapilla*)
3. Laughing Kookaburra (*Dacelo novaeguineae*)
4. Painted Honeyeater (*Grantiella picta*)
5. Australian Boobook (*Ninox boobook*)
6. Swift Parrot (*Lathamus discolor*)
7. **Southern Bent-wing Bat (*Miniopterus orianae*)**
8. **Tawny Frogmouth (*Podargus strigoides*)**
9. **Spotted Marsh Frog (*Limnodynastes tasmaniensis*)**
10. Eastern Barred Bandicoot (*Perameles gunnii*)
11. Tussock Skink (*Pseudemoia pagenstecheri*)
12. **Short-beaked Echidna (*Tachyglossus aculeatus*)**
13. Bush Stone-curlew (*Burhinus grallarius*)
14. **Growling Grass Frog (*Litoria raniformis*)**
15. Common Eastern Froglet (*Crinia signifera*)
16. White-winged Chough (*Corcorax melanorhamphos*)
17. Willie Wagtail (*Rhipidura leucophrys*)
18. **Eastern Yellow Robin (*Eopsaltria australis*)**
19. Superb Fairywren (*Malurus cyaneus*)
20. Australian Painted Lady (*Vanessa kershawi*)
21. **Plains-wanderer (*Pedionomus torquatus*)**
22. Eastern Blue-tongued Skink (*Tiliqua scincoides*)
23. Striped Legless Lizard (*Delma impar*)
24. **Fat-tailed Dunnart (*Sminthopsis crassicaudata*)**
25. **Little Whip Snake (*Suta flagellum*)**
26. **Victorian Grassland Earless Dragon (*Tympanocryptis pinguicolla*)**
27. Golden Sun Moth (*Synemon plana*)
28. False Garden Mantid (*Pseudomantis albofimbriata*)

DARWIN HARBOUR MANGROVES

1. **Little Red Flying-fox (*Pteropus scapulatus*)**
2. Magpie Goose (*Anseranas semipalmata*)
3. **Mangrove Monitor (*Varanus indicus*)**
4. **Canary White-eye (*Zosterops luteus*)**
5. Curlew Sandpiper (*Calidris ferruginea*)
6. White-breasted Whistler (*Pachycephala lanioides*)
7. Mangrove Robin (*Peneothello pulverulenta*)
8. **Chestnut Rail (*Eulabeornis castaneoventris*)**
9. **Giant Mud Crab (*Scylla serrata*)**
10. Beach Stone-curlew (*Esacus magnirostris*)
11. Eastern Curlew (*Numenius madagascariensis*)
12. Pied Oystercatcher (*Haematopus longirostris*)
13. Bar-tailed Godwit (*Limosa lapponica*)
14. Saltwater Crocodile (*Crocodylus porosus*)
15. Hairy-handed Fiddler Crab (*Tubuca hirsutimanus*)
16. Mud Mussels (*Geloina expansa*)
17. **Black-ringed Mangrove Sea Snake (*Hydrelaps darwiniensis*)**
18. Olive Ridley Turtle (*Lepidochelys olivacea*)
19. Mangrove Golden Whistler (*Pachycephala melanura*)
20. Saucer Scallop (*Amusium pleuronectes*)
21. Long Bum (*Telescopium telescopium*)
22. Flatback Turtle (*Natator depressus*)
23. Mangrove Jack (*Lutjanus argentimaculatus*)
24. Copper Jewel butterfly (*Hypochrysops apelles*)
25. **Hooded Katydid (*Phyllophorella queenslandica*)**
26. **Darwin's Mudskipper (*Periophthalmus darwini*)**
27. Graphic Flutterer Dragonfly (*Rhyothemis graphiptera*)
28. Barramundi (*Lates calcarifer*)
29. **Thin Periwinkle (*Littoraria filosa*)**
30. **Blue Threadfin (*Eleutheronema tetradactylum*)**

ANTARCTICA

1 South Polar Skua (*Stercorarius maccormicki*)
2. **Crabeater Seal (*Lobodon carcinophaga*)**
3. **Snow Petrel (*Pagodroma nivea*)**
4. Snowy Albatross (*Diomedea exulans*)
5. Humpback Whale (*Megaptera novaeangliae*)
6. **Antarctic Tern (*Sterna vittata*)**
7. Light-mantled Albatross (*Phoebetria palpebrata*)
8. **Snowy Sheathbill (*Chionis albus*)**
9. Emperor Penguin (*Aptenodytes forsteri*)
10. Southern Fulmar (*Fulmarus glacialoides*)
11. **Macaroni Penguin (*Eudyptes chrysolophus*)**
12. Ross Seal (*Ommatophoca rossii*)
13. Orca (*Orcinus orca*)
14. **Antarctic Minke Whale (*Balaenoptera bonaerensis*)**
15. **Imperial Cormorant (*Leucocarbo atriceps*)**
16. Gentoo Penguin (*Pygoscelis papua*)
17. Chinstrap Penguin (*Pygoscelis antarcticus*)
18. Kelp Gull (*Larus dominicanus*)
19. Antarctic Krill (*Euphausia superba*)
20. Antarctic Cod (*Dissostichus mawsoni*)
21. Wilson's Storm Petrel (*Oceanites oceanicus*)
22. Weddell Seal (*Leptonychotes weddellii*)
23. **Unicorn Icefish (*Channichthys rhinoceratus*)**
24. Southern Elephant Seal (*Mirounga leonina*)
25. **Patagonian Toothfish (*Dissostichus eleginoides*)**
26. **Leopard Seal (*Hydrurga leptonyx*)**
27. Colossal Squid (*Mesonychoteuthis hamiltoni*)
28. Blue Whale (*Balaenoptera musculus*)

SOIL

1. Giant Burrowing Frog (*Heleioporus australiacus*)
2. **Green-head Ant (*Rhytidoponera metallica*)**
3. **White's Skink (*Liopholis whitii*)**
4. **Giant Velvet Worm (*Tasmanipatus barretti*)**
5. **Sugar Ant (*Camponotus consobrinus*)**
6. Mallacoota Burrowing Crayfish (*Engaeus mallacoota*)
7. **Pobblebonk (*Limnodynastes dumerilii*)**
8. Australian Black Field Cricket (*Teleogryllus commodus*)
9. Victorian Grassland Earless Dragon (*Tympanocryptis pinguicolla*)
10. Common Earthworm (*Aporrectodea caliginosa*)
11. **Greengrocer Cicada (*Cyclochila australasiae*)**
12. Mole Cricket (*Gryllotalpa* sp.)
13. **Common Slater (*Porcellio scaber*)**
14. Wishbone Spider (*Aname* sp.)
15. **Striped Legless Lizard (*Delma impar*)**
16. Bull Ant (*Myrmecia pyriformis*)
17. Scarab Beetle larvae (Scarabaeidae)
18. Scarab Beetle larvae (Scarabaeidae)
19. Symphyla
20. **Red Velvet Mite (Trombidiidae)**
21. **Black Portuguese Millipede (*Ommatoiulus moreleti*)**
22. Springtail (Collembola)
23. Proximus Blind Snake (*Anilios proximus*)
24. Two-pronged Bristletails (Diplura)
25. Meat Ant (*Iridomyrmex purpureus*)
26. Giant Gippsland Earthworm (*Megascolides australis*)
27. Giant Northern Termite (*Mastotermes darwiniensis*)

THE GRAMPIANS

1. **White-striped Free-tailed Bat (*Austronomus australis*)**
2. Eastern Ring-tailed Possum (*Pseudocheirus peregrinus*)
3. Krefft's Glider (*Petaurus notatus*)
4. Crimson Rosella (*Platycercus elegans*)
5. Whistling Kite (*Haliastur sphenurus*)
6. **Wedge-tailed Eagle (*Aquila audax*)**
7. Red-tailed Black Cockatoo (*Calyptorhynchus banksii*)
8. Galah (*Eolophus roseicapilla*)
9. **Spotted Pardalote (*Pardalotus punctatus*)**
10. **Eastern Pygmy Possum (*Cercartetus nanus*)**
11. Powerful Owl (*Ninox strenua*)
12. Eastern Grey Kangaroo (*Macropus giganteus*)
13. Swamp Wallaby (*Wallabia bicolor*)
14. Koala (*Phascolarctos cinereus*)
15. **Lace Monitor (*Varanus varius*)**
16. Sulphur-crested Cockatoo (*Cacatua galerita*)
17. Lesser Long-eared Bat (*Nyctophilus geoffroyi*)
18. Red-necked Wallaby (*Notamacropus rufogriseus*)
19. Flame Robin (*Petroica phoenicea*)
20. **Eastern Bearded Dragon (*Pogona barbata*)**
21. **Rainbow Lorikeet (*Trichoglossus moluccanus*)**
22. **Tiger Snake (*Notechis scutatus*)**
23. Brush-tailed Rock Wallaby (*Petrogale penicillata*)
24. **Common Brush-tailed Possum (*Trichosurus vulpecula*)**
25. Long-nosed Potoroo (*Potorous tridactylus*)
26. **Smoky Mouse (*Pseudomys fumeus*)**
27. Red-bellied Black Snake (*Pseudechis porphyriacus*)
28. Eastern Three-lined Skink (*Acritoscincus duperreyi*)
29. Southern Brown Bandicoot (*Isoodon obesulus*)
30. Narrow-toed Feather-tailed Glider (*Acrobates pygmaeus*)

Did you find all 80 hidden animals? Amazing! But there's more to see ...

Once you've found all of the hidden animals, why not try setting your own challenges? There are some examples below to get you started.

How many things with wings can you spot in the Gibson Desert?

How many furry friends can you see in the Grampians?

How many different types of flowers can you find in the Victorian Volcanic Plain?

There are eight diverse biomes featured in this book, but many more environments exist—even in our own backyards!

Next time you go outside, see what types of habitats you can spot. Local parks and pockets of nature, even in cities and towns, can be home to all kinds of plants and animals. Look closer ... what can you find?

First published in 2025 by
Museums Victoria Publishing
11 Nicholson Street
Carlton, Victoria 3053, Australia
publications@museum.vic.gov.au
www.museumsvictoria.com.au

A catalogue record for this book is available from the National Library of Australia

ISBN 9781921833731

Design by Julia Donkersley
Production by Sasha Beekman
Text by Sasha Beekman, Miriam Capper and Kate Phillips

MIX
Paper | Supporting responsible forestry
FSC® C144853

Printed in China by RR Donnelley Asia Printing Solutions, Ltd.

1 3 5 7 9 10 8 6 4 2

Many thanks to the collection managers, curators and researchers from the Museums Victoria Research Institute, whose guidance and expertise informed this book.

Museums Victoria acknowledges the Wurundjeri Woi Wurrung and Boon Wurrung peoples of the eastern Kulin Nations where we work, and First Peoples language groups and communities across Victoria and Australia. Our organisation, in partnership with the First Peoples of Victoria, is working to place First Peoples living cultures and histories at the core of our practice.

This book has been created by Museums Victoria, Australia's largest public museum organisation. Our venues include Melbourne Museum, Scienceworks, Immigration Museum and Royal Exhibition Building. Proceeds from the sale of this book support Museums Victoria's collections and ongoing research.